Squizzy the Black Squirrel

A Fabulous Fable of Friendship

Written by Chuck Stone

Illustrated by Jeannie Jackson

Open Hand Publishing, LLC
Greensboro, North Carolina
www.openhand.com

A black squirrel I did see one day,
Enjoying the lovely weather.
The other squirrels were brown and gray,
But they all played together.

— CHUCK STONE

Dedication

To Charlie: who was an adventuresome eight-year-old in 1974,
when he saw his first black squirrel in Fairmount Park

and

To Parade: now eight, who searches for horizons where black squirrels frolic
with squirrels of different colors

Open Hand Publishing, LLC
P.O. Box 20207
Greensboro, NC 27420
336-292-8585
e-mail: info@openhand.com
www.openhand.com

Book and Cover Design: The Roberts Group

ISBN 0-940880-71-7

Library of Congress Cataloging in Publication Data
Stone, Chuck.
   Squizzy the black squirrel : a fabulous fable of friendship /
written by Chuck Stone ; illustrated by Jeannie Jackson.
      p. cm.
Summary: After talking with Squizzy, the only black squirrel in Fairmount Park, a young
African-American boy learns that using color to describe one's friends is silly.
   ISBN 0-940880-71-7
   [1. Race awareness—Fiction. 2. Friendship—Fiction. 3. Squirrels—Fiction.
4. African-Americans—Fiction. 5. Fables.] I. Jackson, Jeannie, 1942– ill. II. Title.
   PZ8.2.S875 Sq 2003
   [E]—dc21

                    2003046488

FIRST EDITION — 2003

Printed in Korea
07 06 05 04 03   5 4 3 2 1

Hi, my name is Marcus.
I am seven years old,
and I go to Jim Shumaker
Elementary School.

1

My second grade teacher, Miss Dunphy, always tells us to try to make a new friend every year.

But how do you make a new friend when you live on the same street and go to the same school and see all the same kids all the time?

How would I ever make a new friend?

Then, one day, I got a surprise. I was playing with some friends in Fairmount Park, where a lot of squirrels live, and I saw a black squirrel.

He was sitting beside a tree. Other squirrels—one was red and the others looked brown or gray—were playing in the tree's branches above, but he was the only black squirrel.

I had never seen a black squirrel before. Gee, wouldn't it be nice if I could talk to him?

But every
time I got
close,
he would run
up the tree to
play with the
other
squirrels.

One day, he fooled me.

He did not run away. He just stopped. He turned around and looked straight . . .

. . . at me.

"What do you want?" he asked in a squeaky voice. (My mother told me that squirrels talk in squeaky voices, just like bears talk in growly voices.)

"Why do you keep coming near my oak tree?" he asked. "Leave me alone." He sounded real angry.

"I'm sorry," I said. "But, gee, I never saw a black squirrel before. You're cool."

9

"I am not 'cool'," he said. "I am a SQUIRREL!" His tail went straight up and began wiggling back and forth.

"Yeah, but you are a BLACK squirrel."

"I am a SQUIRREL!" he shouted again in his squeaky voice. He was getting more angry and his little whiskers began twitching very fast.

He climbed a tree
and turned back
toward me.

"Besides," he asked,
"what's a 'black'?"

"Black is a color."

"What is a color?
Can a color gather
acorns?"

"No, of course not."

11

"Can it run up trees and jump from branch to branch?"

"No, and you're being silly. I already told you that black is only a color."

"I still don't understand what a 'black' or a 'color' is. I know what a SQUIRREL is and I can tell you what one does."

"I want to know, too. Please tell me."

"A squirrel plays with other squirrels. We gather acorns all day and bury them in the ground.

"After snow covers the ground . . .

. . . we always have something to eat."

"When it gets warm again and the robins come back, we chase each other and have lots of fun."

"I know you have fun. And I saw you doing all the same things that—that—well, that the other squirrels do.

"But you're the only black squirrel in the w-h-o-l-e park. Like, look at me. I'm black."

"You're just a little boy. You're like all the little kids who play here and let their dogs chase us squirrels. And that's not nice."

"I'm sorry. Their dogs should not chase you. The kids are my good friends and we play together. They're all different colors. Some are black like me, some are white, some are yellow, and some are brown. Their fathers and mothers came from different countries."

"There you go again," he said, "using words I don't understand—'different countries', 'white', 'yellow', 'brown'. Squirrels never say words like that. Do you know why?"

I scrunched up my
shoulders, like we do
in Miss Dunphy's
class when we don't
know the answer. 17

"Because words don't help us squirrels gather acorns. Paws do—uh—what's your name?"

"My name is Marcus."

"Is that all there is? Just Marcus?"

"Well, it really is Marcus Chase Chafin. My friends call me Marky."

"I am glad to meet you, Marcus Chase Chafin. My name is Squizzle Romp Rodent. My friends call me Squizzy."

"I live in these oak trees with my six best friends—
Squeegee, Squanto, Squawly, Squealy . . .

. . . Squibly, and Squishy."

"But, Squizzy, you're still the only BLACK squirrel in the w-h-o-l-e park and the other squirrels don't even seem to care that you're different."

"Marky, you keep on saying that word, 'black'. Let's ask my best friend, Squeegee, what it means."

"Hey, Squeegee, what's a black squirrel?"

Squeegee stopped. Her paw scratched her head and her whiskers twitched. She frowned and said in a squeaky voice, "Squizzy, are you acorns?" (That's squirrel talk for, are you nuts?) "There is no such thing as a 'BLACK squirrel'. There are only squirrels. I'm a squirrel. You're a squirrel. We are the 'Seven Squirrels'. I have never heard of 'black'."

Squizzy laughed. "Me neither, Squeegee. Marcus says he's got friends who are—here are some other words—white, brown, black, and yellow.

"He says they're 'different'."

"But Marcus says he's black, just like me. How about this? If he's like me, how come he can't run up and down oak trees and gather acorns like I do?"

Squizzy thought that was so funny, he started laughing. He climbed down the tree and he laughed so hard, he fell back on the ground and kicked his feet in the air. The other squirrels heard him laughing and they started laughing, too.

24

That hurt my feelings because they were making fun of me. I started walking home.

Squizzy yelled, "Hey, Marcus, look!"
I turned around.

The Seven Squirrels—Squanto, Squawky, Squealy, Squibly, Squishy, Squeegee, and Squizzy—were all standing in a line.

They were wiggling their tails and waving their paws at me.

Their front teeth looked like they were grinning.

"Marcus!" they all yelled in their squeaky voices.
"We like you. Please come back and be our friend."

I smiled. Miss Dunphy would be so happy
that I had made more than a new friend,
I had made seven new friends.

And I learned something new, too.

28

All of the squirrels in Fairmount Park are different colors—gray, brown, and red. But only one of them is black.

And they don't even care.

Now, that is really cool because the Seven Squirrels are like me and my friends—all different colors.

Maybe I can't run up and down the trees like Squizzy. Maybe I can't gather acorns like they do.

But . . .

There's a swing near Squizzy's tree, and I can swing way, way up high.

Squizzy sits on my leg and we swing together.

His six friends all wait their turn. And they swing with me, because now they're my friends too.